Shadows of Destruction: The World's Most Devastating Cataclysms

Introduction

Throughout history, moments of unimaginable destruction have reshaped our world, testing the resilience of civilizations and altering the course of human destiny. From devastating earthquakes and towering tsunamis to cataclysmic fires and industrial disasters, these tragic events have repeatedly pushed communities to the brink, reminding us of the relentless power of nature and the dangers of human error. Yet, they have also revealed humanity's remarkable capacity to survive, rebuild, and adapt.

Shadows of Destruction: The World's Most Devastating Cataclysms takes you on a journey through 100 of the most catastrophic events in recorded history. This collection explores each disaster in vivid detail – the moments leading up to it, the chaos it unleashed, and the extraordinary stories of survival and recovery that followed. Each chapter presents an in-depth look at an event that transformed lives and landscapes forever, inviting readers to understand not only what happened, but why it happened and what we have learned as a result.

From the deadly tsunami that swept across the Indian Ocean in 2004 to the explosion at Chernobyl that left a city abandoned, each story in this book reflects the profound impact that these disasters have had on humanity. These events serve as sobering reminders of our world's fragility, highlighting the importance of preparedness, the need for sustainable practices, and the urgency of building resilience in an increasingly interconnected world.

In exploring these shadows of destruction, this book also sheds light on the steps we have taken to prevent history from repeating itself. Improved early warning systems, stronger building codes, advances in disaster response, and growing awareness of climate change are all part of the ongoing legacy of these tragic events. By understanding the roots of each disaster and its long-lasting effects, we gain insight into how far we have come – and how far we still have to go – in our efforts to coexist with the powerful forces that shape our planet.

Shadows of Destruction is not only a tribute to the countless lives impacted by these catastrophes but also a call to action. As we look back on these events, may we remember their lessons, honor the resilience they reveal, and embrace our collective responsibility to build a safer, more prepared world for future generations.

Contents of the book:

1. The 2004 Indian Ocean Earthquake and Tsunami

Location and Date: December 26, 2004; epicenter off the west coast of northern Sumatra, Indonesia
Event Details: A magnitude 9.1–9.3 undersea earthquake struck off the coast, triggering one of the deadliest tsunamis in recorded history.
Cause: Tectonic plate movement in the Indian Ocean, specifically the subduction of the Indo-Australian plate under the Eurasian plate.
Consequences: Estimated 230,000–280,000 fatalities across 14 countries, with Indonesia, Thailand, Sri Lanka, and India being hardest hit. Infrastructure, homes, and coastal ecosystems were destroyed, leading to billions of dollars in damages.
Measures Taken: An Indian Ocean tsunami warning system was established, with seismic monitoring stations, and early warning protocols to better alert residents in case of future events.

2. The Chernobyl Nuclear Disaster

Location and Date: April 26, 1986; Pripyat, Ukraine
Event Details: A nuclear reactor at the Chernobyl power plant exploded, releasing large amounts of radioactive material into the atmosphere.
Cause: A flawed reactor design and operator error during a safety test caused an uncontrolled nuclear reaction, leading to a catastrophic explosion.
Consequences: Approximately 31 direct fatalities, with long-term effects on thousands more due to radiation exposure. Large areas became uninhabitable, resulting in the forced relocation of over 300,000 people.
Measures Taken: The reactor was enclosed in a concrete sarcophagus, and safety protocols were revamped globally. The disaster underscored the importance of strict safety measures and disaster response plans in nuclear energy.

3. The Great Chinese Famine

Location and Date: 1959–1961; People's Republic of China

Event Details: A combination of government policy, environmental factors, and mismanagement led to one of the deadliest famines in human history.

Cause: Policies under the Great Leap Forward, including forced collectivization and unrealistic agricultural quotas, led to a sharp decline in food production. Drought and flood worsened the situation.

Consequences: An estimated 15–45 million deaths due to starvation and malnutrition.

Measures Taken: The famine highlighted the need for agricultural reforms, eventually leading to policy changes and the eventual introduction of the Household Responsibility System, which incentivized production by allowing farmers to keep surplus crops.

4. The 2010 Haiti Earthquake

Location and Date: January 12, 2010; near Port-au-Prince, Haiti

Event Details: A magnitude 7.0 earthquake devastated the Haitian capital and surrounding areas.

Cause: Movement along the Enriquillo–Plantain Garden fault zone, which runs through the Caribbean plate boundary.

Consequences: Over 230,000 fatalities, 300,000 injuries, and over 1 million people displaced. Destruction of infrastructure, including government buildings, homes, and hospitals.

Measures Taken: International relief efforts were mobilized, and stronger building codes were promoted to improve structural resilience in future earthquakes.

5. The Dust Bowl

Location and Date: 1930s; Great Plains, United States
Event Details: Severe dust storms swept through the Great Plains, devastating agriculture and causing mass displacement.
Cause: Poor agricultural practices, severe drought, and high winds eroded topsoil, resulting in vast dust storms.
Consequences: Crop failure, economic devastation, and the migration of approximately 2.5 million people, known as "Okies," many of whom moved to California.
Measures Taken: The U.S. government introduced soil conservation practices, and agricultural policies aimed to prevent future over-farming, like crop rotation and terracing.

6. The 2011 Fukushima Nuclear Disaster

Location and Date: March 11, 2011; Fukushima Prefecture, Japan
Event Details: A massive earthquake and tsunami struck Japan, leading to a meltdown at the Fukushima Daiichi Nuclear Power Plant.
Cause: A 9.0 earthquake and 15-meter tsunami flooded the plant, disabling cooling systems and causing reactor meltdowns.
Consequences: Mass evacuation of nearby residents, contamination of land and water, and long-term health and environmental risks.
Measures Taken: Japan implemented stricter nuclear safety standards and created advanced tsunami defenses. Globally, nuclear plants re-evaluated their disaster readiness.

7. Mount Tambora Eruption

Location and Date: April 10, 1815; Sumbawa, Indonesia
Event Details: One of the largest volcanic eruptions in recorded history, it altered global weather patterns and caused a "volcanic winter."
Cause: A massive explosive eruption, releasing ash and sulfur dioxide into the atmosphere.
Consequences: Estimated 71,000 deaths, with many succumbing to starvation and disease following agricultural collapse. The "Year Without a Summer" led to global food shortages and economic hardship.
Measures Taken: Improved volcanic monitoring, particularly in regions prone to eruptions, and increased awareness of climate impacts from volcanic activity.

8. The Spanish Flu Pandemic

Location and Date: 1918–1920; worldwide
Event Details: An influenza pandemic infected one-third of the global population, resulting in high mortality.
Cause: A highly contagious H1N1 influenza virus spread rapidly, exacerbated by troop movements and poor medical knowledge during WWI.
Consequences: Estimated 50–100 million deaths globally, overwhelming healthcare systems and causing long-term socioeconomic effects.
Measures Taken: Modern public health practices were influenced by the pandemic, leading to advances in virology and the establishment of influenza surveillance programs.

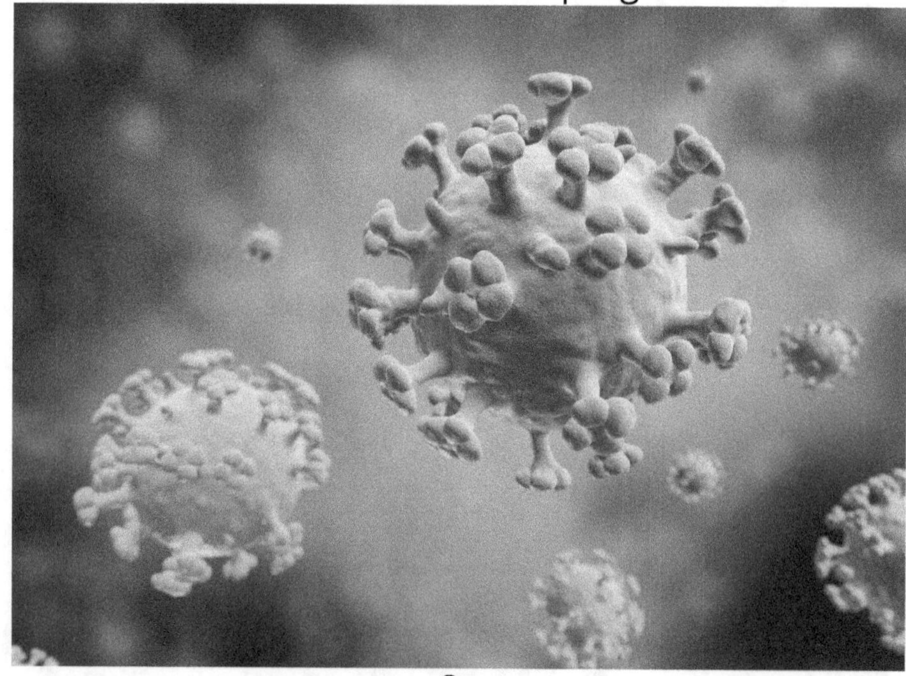

9. Pompeii and Mount Vesuvius Eruption

Location and Date: August 24, 79 AD; Pompeii, Italy

Event Details: The eruption of Mount Vesuvius buried the Roman cities of Pompeii and Herculaneum under volcanic ash.

Cause: Vesuvius's eruption was triggered by the buildup of pressure within the Earth's crust due to tectonic activity.

Consequences: Thousands of deaths, with cities preserved under ash for centuries. The eruption highlighted the dangers of volcanic regions.

Measures Taken: Volcanology advanced as a field, and the city of Naples, near Vesuvius, now has evacuation plans and monitoring systems in place.

10. Hurricane Katrina

Location and Date: August 2005; U.S. Gulf Coast, primarily New Orleans
Event Details: One of the most destructive hurricanes in U.S. history, Katrina caused widespread flooding, especially in New Orleans.
Cause: A category 5 hurricane made landfall, and poorly maintained levees failed, exacerbating the flooding.
Consequences: Over 1,800 deaths, mass displacement, and an estimated $125 billion in damages. Extensive social and economic impacts, with many communities still recovering years later.
Measures Taken: The U.S. Army Corps of Engineers rebuilt levees, and FEMA reformed disaster response practices. Flood defenses and emergency management protocols were improved in vulnerable areas.

11. The Great Lisbon Earthquake

Location and Date: November 1, 1755; Lisbon, Portugal

Event Details: A massive earthquake estimated to be around 8.5–9.0 in magnitude struck Lisbon, followed by a tsunami and fires that devastated the city.

Cause: The earthquake resulted from tectonic activity at the Azores-Gibraltar fault zone, which marks the boundary between the African and Eurasian plates.

Consequences: The earthquake and ensuing tsunami waves up to 20 meters high killed an estimated 30,000–50,000 people, with around 85% of Lisbon's buildings destroyed, including important cultural landmarks. Fires raged for days afterward, worsening the destruction.

Measures Taken: The Marquis of Pombal, Portugal's prime minister, led rebuilding efforts, employing earthquake-resistant architecture in Lisbon and conducting one of the first seismological studies. These early efforts inspired modern earthquake engineering and risk management.

12. The Black Death

Location and Date: 1347–1351; Europe, Asia, and North Africa

Event Details: The bubonic plague pandemic, often called the Black Death, swept across continents, killing a significant portion of the global population.

Cause: The disease, caused by the bacterium Yersinia pestis, spread primarily through fleas on rats. It was exacerbated by poor hygiene, crowded cities, and a lack of medical knowledge.

Consequences: An estimated 75–200 million people died, with Europe losing 30–60% of its population. The social and economic fabric of Europe changed drastically, weakening feudalism, causing labor shortages, and sparking new waves of persecution, especially against marginalized groups.

Measures Taken: In its aftermath, cities developed basic public health measures, including quarantine and sanitation practices. The concept of "quarantine" itself was formalized in Venice in response to the plague.

13. Typhoon Haiyan

Location and Date: November 8, 2013; Philippines, especially Leyte and Samar islands

Event Details: Known locally as Super Typhoon Yolanda, Haiyan was one of the strongest tropical cyclones recorded at landfall, causing catastrophic damage.

Cause: The typhoon's intensity was due to warm ocean temperatures and favorable atmospheric conditions, amplified by climate change, which increases the frequency of extreme weather events.

Consequences: Over 6,300 fatalities and massive destruction of infrastructure. Entire communities were leveled, with over 1 million homes destroyed and widespread shortages of food, water, and medical supplies.

Measures Taken: Improved forecasting and communication systems were implemented in the Philippines. Evacuation protocols were strengthened, and the disaster highlighted the global need for climate change adaptation to reduce the severity of such events.

14. The 1906 San Francisco Earthquake

Location and Date: April 18, 1906; San Francisco, California, USA
Event Details: A 7.9 magnitude earthquake struck the city, resulting in widespread destruction and fires.
Cause: The earthquake occurred along the San Andreas Fault, a transform fault where the Pacific and North American plates slide past each other.
Consequences: The quake and subsequent fires destroyed over 80% of the city and led to approximately 3,000 deaths, with 250,000 people left homeless. Fires ravaged the city for days, causing most of the property damage.
Measures Taken: The earthquake led to advancements in seismic research, and fire codes were established or strengthened to reduce future risks. Building codes across California evolved to ensure greater earthquake resistance.

15. The 1883 Krakatoa Eruption

Location and Date: August 26–27, 1883; Krakatoa, between Java and Sumatra, Indonesia

Event Details: A massive volcanic eruption that obliterated much of the island, with explosions heard as far as 3,000 miles away.

Cause: Pressure built up within the magma chamber, eventually resulting in one of the largest eruptions recorded, with enormous pyroclastic flows and tsunami waves.

Consequences: Over 36,000 people died, primarily due to tsunamis caused by the eruption. The explosion destroyed over two-thirds of the island, and ash caused global temperatures to drop, affecting weather patterns and agriculture for years.

Measures Taken: The eruption led to greater scientific interest in volcanic eruptions, and Indonesia established a system of volcanic observatories to monitor future activity. This eruption also deepened the global understanding of climate effects from volcanic ash.

16. The Great Fire of London

Location and Date: September 2–6, 1666; London, England

Event Details: A fire that started in a bakery on Pudding Lane spread rapidly through London, destroying large parts of the city.

Cause: The fire spread easily due to the dense wooden buildings and narrow streets, as well as the lack of fire-fighting resources.

Consequences: Although only a few deaths were recorded, the fire destroyed 87 churches, 13,200 houses, and many commercial buildings, leaving 70,000–80,000 people homeless.

Measures Taken: Rebuilding plans enforced fire-resistant materials such as brick and stone. The fire led to the establishment of London's first insurance companies and fire brigades, creating modern firefighting and urban planning standards.

17. The 1811–1812 New Madrid Earthquakes

Location and Date: December 1811–February 1812; New Madrid, Missouri, USA

Event Details: A series of powerful earthquakes along the New Madrid Seismic Zone, with aftershocks felt across the eastern United States.

Cause: The New Madrid fault, an intraplate fault zone within the North American tectonic plate, triggered these quakes.

Consequences: Though sparsely populated at the time, the earthquakes changed the course of the Mississippi River and caused temporary waterfalls and lakes to form. The events damaged settlements and led to economic loss in the region.

Measures Taken: Research and monitoring in the New Madrid Seismic Zone continue today to anticipate future earthquakes, and building codes in surrounding areas were adjusted to account for seismic risk.

18. The 1931 China Floods

Location and Date: Summer 1931; primarily the Yangtze River basin, China

Event Details: Known as one of the deadliest natural disasters in recorded history, the floods caused widespread destruction and loss of life.

Cause: A combination of heavy rains, snowmelt, and the failure of dikes along the Yangtze, Huai, and Yellow Rivers.

Consequences: It's estimated that between 1–4 million people died from drowning, disease, and starvation. Millions were displaced, and crops and homes were destroyed, leading to a long-lasting famine.

Measures Taken: The event underscored the importance of flood control infrastructure in China, leading to extensive dike and dam construction, such as the Three Gorges Dam.

19. The 1923 Great Kanto Earthquake

Location and Date: September 1, 1923; Kanto region, Japan, primarily Tokyo and Yokohama

Event Details: A 7.9 magnitude earthquake devastated the Kanto region, followed by widespread fires and a powerful typhoon that complicated recovery.

Cause: Tectonic movements along the Sagami Trough, which lies between the Philippine Sea and the Eurasian plates.

Consequences: Approximately 142,000 fatalities, with large sections of Tokyo and Yokohama destroyed by fire. Social and political unrest followed, leading to increased anti-Korean sentiments and violence against marginalized communities.

Measures Taken: Japan began developing earthquake-resistant buildings, especially in Tokyo, and strengthened disaster preparedness programs. The anniversary of the quake became Disaster Prevention Day in Japan.

20. The 2019–2020 Australian Bushfires ("Black Summer")

Location and Date: June 2019–May 2020; various regions across Australia

Event Details: Massive wildfires burned millions of acres across the continent, with severe consequences for wildlife, people, and ecosystems.

Cause: A combination of prolonged drought, extreme heat, and climate change, with fires ignited both naturally and by human actions.

Consequences: At least 33 people died, with over 3,000 homes destroyed. An estimated 3 billion animals were affected, with some species pushed closer to extinction. The economic cost reached billions of dollars, impacting tourism, health, and agriculture.

Measures Taken: Australia committed to more stringent fire management practices, including controlled burns and firebreaks. The event fueled discussions around climate action to address conditions exacerbating wildfire risk.

21. Hurricane Maria

Location and Date: September 16–30, 2017; primarily Puerto Rico, Dominica, and U.S. Virgin Islands

Event Details: A Category 5 hurricane that caused unprecedented devastation, particularly in Puerto Rico.

Cause: Warm ocean waters and favorable atmospheric conditions intensified Maria to Category 5 strength, with climate change contributing to the hurricane's severity.

Consequences: Over 3,000 fatalities, most due to indirect causes such as power outages, lack of access to medical care, and clean water shortages. Damage exceeded $90 billion, with widespread destruction of homes, infrastructure, and ecosystems.

Measures Taken: Post-Maria, Puerto Rico has focused on modernizing its power grid, improving emergency response, and increasing resilience to future storms. FEMA implemented new disaster response protocols, and there has been a push for climate-resilient infrastructure.

22. California Wildfires (2018)

Location and Date: Throughout 2018; California, USA
Event Details: Wildfires fueled by drought, dry vegetation, and high winds burned millions of acres across California.

Cause: Climate change, prolonged drought, and utility equipment malfunctions contributed to the fires. One of the largest was the Camp Fire, which began due to a spark from power lines.

Consequences: Over 100 fatalities, with around 18,000 structures destroyed in the Camp Fire alone, which nearly wiped out the town of Paradise. The financial losses were estimated at over $16 billion, and the fires contributed to poor air quality across the western U.S.

Measures Taken: California has implemented stricter regulations for utility companies, expanded firefighting resources, and increased funding for forest management, such as controlled burns and vegetation clearing. Additionally, there are enhanced public alert systems for high-risk fire conditions.

23. The 2015 Nepal Earthquake

Location and Date: April 25, 2015; near Kathmandu, Nepal

Event Details: A magnitude 7.8 earthquake struck Nepal, causing extensive damage in the Kathmandu Valley.

Cause: Tectonic activity along the collision boundary between the Indian and Eurasian plates, where pressure buildup over decades led to the quake.

Consequences: Over 9,000 fatalities and more than 22,000 injuries. Historic sites, homes, and infrastructure were heavily damaged, with approximately 3.5 million people displaced.

Measures Taken: Nepal received international aid, and the earthquake highlighted the need for earthquake-resistant construction practices. Reconstruction efforts focused on resilient structures and rebuilding cultural sites. Additionally, Nepal has developed improved disaster response systems to better handle future events.

24. Cyclone Idai

Location and Date: March 4–21, 2019; primarily Mozambique, Zimbabwe, and Malawi

Event Details: One of the worst tropical cyclones to strike the Southern Hemisphere, causing widespread flooding and destruction.

Cause: Warm waters and favorable conditions in the Mozambique Channel led to Cyclone Idai's formation and intensification, with climate change heightening storm severity.

Consequences: Approximately 1,300 deaths and massive flooding that displaced hundreds of thousands. Cities such as Beira in Mozambique were submerged, and food insecurity affected millions due to destroyed crops and infrastructure.

Measures Taken: International agencies supported the affected areas with relief aid and rebuilding efforts. Mozambique and neighboring countries worked on improving early warning systems, disaster management plans, and climate-resilient infrastructure.

25. The 2011 Joplin Tornado

Location and Date: May 22, 2011; Joplin, Missouri, USA

Event Details: An EF5 tornado with wind speeds exceeding 200 mph devastated the city of Joplin.

Cause: A severe thunderstorm created the ideal conditions for a tornado, with a strong jet stream and wind shear contributing to its intensity.

Consequences: The tornado caused 158 fatalities and injured over 1,000 people. About 7,500 buildings were destroyed, with estimated damages of $2.8 billion. Joplin's infrastructure, schools, and homes were leveled, creating long-term impacts on the community.

Measures Taken: Joplin invested in advanced early warning systems, and new building codes were adopted for tornado resistance. FEMA reviewed and improved emergency response practices, and local programs promoted community preparedness and storm shelters.

26. The 2010 Deepwater Horizon Oil Spill

Location and Date: April 20, 2010; Gulf of Mexico, near Louisiana, USA

Event Details: The Deepwater Horizon oil rig exploded, causing the largest marine oil spill in history.

Cause: The blowout preventer failed during deep-sea drilling by BP, allowing oil to gush into the Gulf for 87 days.

Consequences: Approximately 4.9 million barrels of oil leaked, devastating marine and coastal ecosystems and harming local economies reliant on fishing and tourism. Cleanup costs and economic losses totaled in the tens of billions.

Measures Taken: Stricter drilling regulations were implemented in the U.S., including enhanced safety standards for blowout preventers and deep-sea drilling. BP and other companies invested in improved safety measures, and there was a shift toward alternative energy sources to reduce oil dependency.

27. Typhoon Goni

Location and Date: October 2020; Philippines, primarily Catanduanes and Luzon Island
Event Details: Typhoon Goni (known locally as Rolly) was a Category 5 super typhoon that struck the Philippines, causing extreme destruction.
Cause: Goni intensified over warm Pacific waters before making landfall, driven by atmospheric conditions favorable for a high-intensity storm.
Consequences: Over 20 fatalities, with 425,000 homes damaged or destroyed, and widespread flooding. The storm displaced hundreds of thousands of residents and inflicted severe damage to agriculture and infrastructure.
Measures Taken: The Philippines has worked to strengthen its disaster response and early warning systems. Structural improvements were made in storm-vulnerable regions, and educational campaigns were launched to prepare communities for typhoon season.

28. The 2013 Alberta Floods

Location and Date: June 2013; Southern Alberta, Canada, including Calgary
Event Details: Heavy rainfall and rapid snowmelt led to catastrophic flooding across Southern Alberta.
Cause: A slow-moving weather system brought intense rainfall to already saturated soil, with high mountain snowpack melting quickly due to warm temperatures.
Consequences: An estimated $5 billion in damages, with over 100,000 residents evacuated and significant impacts to Calgary's downtown and infrastructure.
Measures Taken: Alberta invested in new flood defenses, including riverbank stabilization, dams, and reservoirs. An emergency alert system was strengthened, and the city of Calgary developed a flood resilience plan.

29. The 2021 Texas Winter Storm

Location and Date: February 2021; Texas, USA
Event Details: A polar vortex caused a severe winter storm, bringing freezing temperatures and widespread power outages across Texas.
Cause: A breakdown in the polar vortex allowed Arctic air to flow south, bringing extreme cold to regions unprepared for it. Texas's independent power grid failed under the pressure of increased demand and frozen infrastructure.
Consequences: Over 200 fatalities and millions of residents left without power, heat, or water for days. The total economic cost was estimated at $195 billion, as burst pipes and frozen equipment caused widespread damage.
Measures Taken: Texas began winterizing its power grid and critical infrastructure to prevent similar outages. Policy changes were introduced to ensure power providers prepare for extreme weather, and there were calls for increased interconnections with national grids.

30. Cyclone Tauktae

Location and Date: May 14–19, 2021; India, especially Gujarat and Maharashtra

Event Details: Cyclone Tauktae was one of the strongest cyclones to hit India's western coast, causing widespread devastation.

Cause: Unusually warm Arabian Sea waters fueled Tauktae's rapid intensification, exacerbated by climate change.

Consequences: Over 100 fatalities and substantial damage along the coast, including power outages, destroyed buildings, and displaced communities. The cyclone damaged COVID-19 hospitals and disrupted vaccine distribution amid India's pandemic surge.

Measures Taken: India expanded cyclone preparedness measures, strengthened coastal defenses, and enhanced warning systems. Cyclone shelters and evacuation protocols were improved, and there was an increased focus on climate resilience in disaster-prone regions.

31. The 2019 Amazon Rainforest Fires

Location and Date: Primarily June–October 2019; Amazon Basin, mainly Brazil

Event Details: Massive wildfires spread through the Amazon rainforest, exacerbating deforestation and contributing to global carbon emissions.

Cause: Deforestation, illegal logging, and clearing practices for agriculture, combined with dry conditions, led to widespread fires.

Consequences: Millions of hectares of rainforest burned, threatening biodiversity and indigenous communities. The fires released large amounts of CO_2, impacting global climate. The smoke caused respiratory problems in nearby communities.

Measures Taken: Brazil and international organizations increased monitoring efforts, implemented stricter regulations on deforestation, and provided more funding for firefighting. Conservation programs were expanded to protect the Amazon, and calls for sustainable agriculture practices increased.

32. Typhoon Hato

Location and Date: August 23, 2017; Hong Kong, Macau, and South China

Event Details: Typhoon Hato, a Category 10 storm, hit Hong Kong and Macau, causing severe flooding and wind damage.

Cause: Warm ocean waters in the South China Sea intensified the storm, while Hato's direct hit on Macau was rare and destructive.

Consequences: At least 26 deaths, billions of dollars in damages, and large-scale power outages. The storm caused serious economic losses, affecting casinos and businesses in Macau.

Measures Taken: In response, Hong Kong and Macau improved flood defenses, strengthened building codes, and enhanced their storm warning systems. Macau also reinforced its drainage systems to reduce the impact of future typhoons.

33. The 2008 Sichuan Earthquake

Location and Date: May 12, 2008; Sichuan Province, China

Event Details: A magnitude 7.9 earthquake struck Sichuan, causing widespread devastation and loss of life.

Cause: Tectonic activity along the Longmenshan Fault, where the Indian and Eurasian plates collide, triggered the earthquake.

Consequences: Approximately 87,000 fatalities and hundreds of thousands injured. Over 5 million people were displaced, and schools, homes, and infrastructure were severely damaged. The quake had a profound social impact due to the large number of children lost in school collapses.

Measures Taken: China adopted stricter building codes for schools and public infrastructure, increased earthquake monitoring, and enhanced emergency response protocols. Reconstruction efforts emphasized resilience and safety.

34. Cyclone Nargis

Location and Date: May 2–3, 2008; Myanmar, especially the Irrawaddy Delta
Event Details: Cyclone Nargis struck Myanmar, creating catastrophic flooding and destruction in the low-lying delta region.
Cause: Favorable conditions in the Bay of Bengal intensified the cyclone, while low-lying areas of the Irrawaddy Delta were highly vulnerable.
Consequences: Over 138,000 fatalities, with massive destruction to homes, agriculture, and infrastructure. The storm displaced millions and caused severe food shortages.
Measures Taken: Myanmar began to develop more robust disaster management systems, including early warning systems and community evacuation plans. The international community provided support to improve emergency response and strengthen cyclone defenses.

35. The 2018 Sulawesi Earthquake and Tsunami

Location and Date: September 28, 2018; Palu, Sulawesi, Indonesia

Event Details: A magnitude 7.5 earthquake triggered a tsunami that struck Palu, causing catastrophic damage.

Cause: The earthquake occurred along the Palu-Koro fault, with the vertical displacement causing a local tsunami.

Consequences: Approximately 4,340 fatalities, extensive damage to infrastructure, and displacement of thousands. The quake and tsunami caused significant economic loss, particularly in Palu.

Measures Taken: Indonesia expanded its tsunami early warning system, focusing on improving sensors and response time. Structural resilience was prioritized in reconstruction, and community awareness programs were established for earthquake and tsunami preparedness.

36. The 2017 Mexico City Earthquake

Location and Date: September 19, 2017; Mexico City, Mexico

Event Details: A magnitude 7.1 earthquake struck central Mexico, hitting the densely populated Mexico City.

Cause: Mexico's location near multiple tectonic plates, including the Cocos, Pacific, and North American plates, makes it highly susceptible to seismic activity.

Consequences: Around 370 fatalities, thousands injured, and significant structural damage in Mexico City. Buildings, including schools and hospitals, suffered severe damage or collapse, displacing thousands.

Measures Taken: Mexico strengthened its early warning systems, bolstered earthquake-resilient construction practices, and implemented community preparedness programs. Building codes were reviewed, and stricter regulations were enforced in high-risk zones.

37. The 2003 European Heatwave

Location and Date: Summer of 2003; Western and Central Europe

Event Details: An intense heatwave swept across Europe, causing extreme temperatures and drought conditions.

Cause: An unusual weather pattern trapped warm air over Europe, with climate change increasing the frequency and severity of heatwaves.

Consequences: Over 70,000 deaths, primarily among vulnerable populations such as the elderly. Agriculture suffered greatly due to crop failures, and economic losses exceeded €13 billion.

Measures Taken: European countries developed heat action plans, with early warning systems, public cooling centers, and educational programs on heat safety. Urban areas invested in green infrastructure to reduce heat island effects.

38. Cyclone Fani

Location and Date: May 2–3, 2019; Odisha, India, and Bangladesh
Event Details: Cyclone Fani, one of the strongest cyclones to hit Odisha, caused extensive destruction in India and Bangladesh.
Cause: Warm waters in the Bay of Bengal intensified the cyclone, and favorable atmospheric conditions sustained its strength as it approached the coast.
Consequences: Around 89 fatalities, with thousands of homes and buildings damaged or destroyed. Massive economic losses and agricultural devastation affected livelihoods.
Measures Taken: India and Bangladesh have improved their early warning systems, evacuation protocols, and cyclone shelters. Coastal defenses were strengthened, and international collaboration on disaster preparedness increased.

39. The 2014 Mount Ontake Eruption

Location and Date: September 27, 2014; Mount Ontake, Japan

Event Details: Mount Ontake erupted suddenly, catching hikers on the mountain by surprise.

Cause: The eruption was a phreatic explosion caused by the sudden release of steam pressure in the volcanic rocks.

Consequences: 63 fatalities, with several injuries and difficulty in recovery efforts due to the high altitude and ashfall. The event exposed the risks to Japan's many popular hiking areas near active volcanoes.

Measures Taken: Japan implemented more detailed volcanic monitoring systems, and information on volcanic activity was made more accessible to the public. Evacuation drills were conducted for communities near active volcanoes.

40. The 2016 Fort McMurray Wildfire

Location and Date: May 2016; Alberta, Canada
Event Details: A massive wildfire forced the evacuation of Fort McMurray, causing extensive damage to the community.
Cause: The fire was fueled by dry conditions, high winds, and an unusually warm winter, with climate change intensifying wildfire risks.
Consequences: No fatalities directly from the fire, but over 2,400 homes and buildings were destroyed, and around 90,000 residents evacuated. Economic losses reached $9 billion, making it one of Canada's costliest disasters.
Measures Taken: Alberta strengthened its wildfire management systems, with investments in firefighting resources and public awareness. The disaster prompted reviews of urban planning to reduce wildfire risks near communities, and new evacuation protocols were established.

41. The 2007 Greek Wildfires

Location and Date: August 2007; various regions in Greece, especially the Peloponnese

Event Details: A series of wildfires spread across Greece, exacerbated by hot, dry conditions and high winds.

Cause: The fires were likely a combination of arson, dry vegetation, and extreme heat, with climate change playing a role in increasing wildfire risks.

Consequences: Over 84 fatalities and thousands of homes and buildings destroyed. Ancient olive groves and wildlife were severely impacted, with long-term economic effects on agriculture and tourism.

Measures Taken: Greece invested in stronger firefighting resources, early warning systems, and public education on fire prevention. Policies for forest management and land-use planning were also implemented to reduce wildfire risks.

42. The 2009 L'Aquila Earthquake

Location and Date: April 6, 2009; L'Aquila, Abruzzo, Italy
Event Details: A magnitude 6.3 earthquake struck the historic town of L'Aquila, causing severe damage.
Cause: The quake resulted from tectonic activity along the Apennine Mountains, where the African and Eurasian plates meet.
Consequences: Around 308 fatalities, with thousands injured and extensive damage to homes, schools, and cultural heritage sites. The region faced long-term economic setbacks as rebuilding took years.
Measures Taken: Italy improved seismic building codes and increased funding for retrofitting historic buildings in earthquake-prone regions. The Italian government also strengthened emergency response systems for future seismic events.

43. The 2015 Chennai Floods

Location and Date: November–December 2015; Chennai, Tamil Nadu, India

Event Details: Heavy monsoon rains led to unprecedented flooding in Chennai, causing widespread damage and displacement.

Cause: Intense rainfall combined with insufficient drainage, unplanned urbanization, and encroachment on wetlands.

Consequences: Approximately 500 fatalities, and over 1.8 million people displaced. The economic losses were estimated at $3 billion, with severe impacts on infrastructure, businesses, and public health.

Measures Taken: Chennai authorities have since worked on improving flood management, revamping drainage infrastructure, and restoring wetlands and lakes to help absorb floodwater. Urban planning

44. The 2009 Black Saturday Bushfires

Location and Date: February 7, 2009; Victoria, Australia

Event Details: A series of devastating bushfires swept through Victoria on an extremely hot and windy day, causing catastrophic damage.

Cause: Prolonged drought, record-high temperatures, and strong winds created ideal conditions for fires, with some believed to be started by arson.

Consequences: 173 fatalities, with more than 2,000 homes destroyed, and extensive ecological damage, especially to native forests. The economic cost was estimated at over $4 billion.

Measures Taken: Australia updated its fire management policies, improved early warning systems, and introduced a "stay or go" policy to help residents make informed decisions about evacuation. Community fire safety education was expanded.

45. The 2018 Kerala Floods

Location and Date: August 2018; Kerala, India
Event Details: Unusually heavy monsoon rains caused flooding and landslides across Kerala, impacting almost all of its districts.
Cause: Exceptionally high rainfall, coupled with dam releases, led to extensive flooding, with climate change increasing monsoon intensity.
Consequences: Over 483 fatalities, hundreds of thousands displaced, and severe destruction to homes, agriculture, and infrastructure. The estimated economic loss was over $4 billion.
Measures Taken: Kerala invested in flood forecasting, dam management systems, and reforestation programs to reduce runoff. Disaster management plans were enhanced, including community preparedness and emergency response coordination.

46. The 2020 Beirut Port Explosion

Location and Date: August 4, 2020; Beirut, Lebanon
Event Details: A massive explosion, caused by the detonation of ammonium nitrate stored improperly in the port, devastated large parts of Beirut.
Cause: Around 2,750 tons of ammonium nitrate had been stored unsafely for years, igniting after a nearby fire spread.
Consequences: At least 218 fatalities, over 7,000 injuries, and around 300,000 people left homeless. The economic cost exceeded $15 billion, with widespread destruction of homes, hospitals, and businesses.
Measures Taken: The incident sparked global discussions on safe storage and handling of hazardous materials. Lebanon committed to improving regulatory oversight and storage safety measures for dangerous goods, and the international community offered expertise on safety protocols.

47. The 2011 Queensland Floods

Location and Date: December 2010 – January 2011; Queensland, Australia

Event Details: Severe flooding affected most of Queensland, causing widespread damage to infrastructure, agriculture, and communities.

Cause: Heavy rain from a strong La Niña event, combined with saturated soils and overflowing rivers, led to extensive flooding.

Consequences: 33 fatalities, with an estimated $2.38 billion in damages, and over 200,000 people affected. Homes, farmlands, and public infrastructure were severely impacted.

Measures Taken: Queensland updated its flood management strategies, built or upgraded levees, and improved flood warning systems. Emergency response training and community education on flood preparedness were expanded.

48. The 2014 West Africa Ebola Outbreak

Location and Date: December 2013 – June 2016; primarily Guinea, Liberia, and Sierra Leone

Event Details: The largest Ebola outbreak in history, which spread across West Africa, overwhelming health systems.

Cause: Ebola virus transmission in highly populated areas, with insufficient healthcare infrastructure to contain the spread.

Consequences: Over 11,000 fatalities, significant loss of healthcare workers, and devastating economic impacts on affected countries. Healthcare systems were strained to breaking points, affecting broader public health.

Measures Taken: The WHO developed stronger protocols for outbreak response, including rapid deployment of medical teams and enhanced contact tracing. Ebola vaccines were developed and deployed, and public health infrastructure was strengthened in affected regions.

49. The 2011 Tohoku Earthquake and Tsunami

Location and Date: March 11, 2011; off the coast of northeastern Japan

Event Details: A magnitude 9.1 earthquake triggered a massive tsunami, leading to the Fukushima Daiichi nuclear disaster.

Cause: Tectonic activity along the Japan Trench, with the Pacific Plate subducting under the North American Plate, caused the earthquake and tsunami.

Consequences: Over 15,000 fatalities, 6,000 injuries, and widespread destruction along the Tohoku coast. The Fukushima nuclear disaster led to evacuations, long-term radiation concerns, and impacts on Japan's energy policy.

Measures Taken: Japan re-evaluated its nuclear safety protocols, strengthened earthquake-resistant building codes, and enhanced early warning systems for earthquakes and tsunamis. Globally, nuclear plants increased their disaster resilience protocols.

50. The 2010 Pakistan Floods

Location and Date: July–September 2010; primarily Pakistan's Indus River basin
Event Details: Heavy monsoon rains caused widespread flooding across Pakistan, displacing millions and devastating communities.
Cause: Unprecedented monsoon rainfall combined with melting glaciers and lack of adequate flood control infrastructure.
Consequences: Approximately 1,985 fatalities, with over 20 million people affected. The flood destroyed crops, homes, and infrastructure, with damages estimated at $10 billion.
Measures Taken: Pakistan invested in flood forecasting, dam infrastructure, and emergency response plans. International aid focused on flood resilience and climate adaptation, while community education on disaster preparedness increased.

51. The 2018 Camp Fire

Location and Date: November 2018; Butte County, California, USA

Event Details: The deadliest wildfire in California's history, which nearly destroyed the entire town of Paradise.

Cause: Dry conditions, strong winds, and a spark from a power line combined to ignite the fire. Climate change played a role by increasing drought frequency.

Consequences: 85 fatalities, over 18,000 structures destroyed, and around 50,000 residents evacuated. Economic losses were estimated at $16.5 billion.

Measures Taken: California increased investments in fire prevention, such as controlled burns and vegetation management. Utility companies implemented power shutoff policies during high-risk conditions, and urban planning strategies were revised to improve wildfire resistance.

52. The 2022 Pakistan Floods

Location and Date: June–October 2022; Pakistan, primarily the Indus River Basin
Event Details: Severe monsoon rains led to record-breaking flooding, impacting a third of the country.
Cause: Climate change intensified monsoon patterns, with inadequate drainage and deforestation contributing to flood severity.
Consequences: Over 1,700 fatalities and more than 33 million people affected. Infrastructure, agriculture, and homes were heavily damaged, leading to an estimated economic loss of $30 billion.
Measures Taken: Pakistan increased international collaboration on climate resilience, invested in flood-resistant infrastructure, and introduced policies for forest and wetland restoration to help manage water runoff.

53. The 2019 Hurricane Dorian

Location and Date: August–September 2019; The Bahamas, U.S. East Coast

Event Details: A Category 5 hurricane that stalled over the Bahamas, causing unprecedented destruction.

Cause: Warm ocean waters and favorable atmospheric conditions allowed Dorian to intensify, with climate change contributing to the storm's unusual behavior.

Consequences: At least 84 fatalities, with thousands left homeless in the Bahamas. Severe flooding, wind damage, and infrastructure loss devastated the islands.

Measures Taken: The Bahamas has invested in climate adaptation, improved hurricane warning systems, and is working on resilient building codes. The event sparked discussions about climate migration and coastal adaptation in the Caribbean.

54. The 2018 Laos Dam Collapse

Location and Date: July 23, 2018; Attapeu Province, Laos

Event Details: The collapse of a dam under construction released billions of cubic meters of water, flooding villages downstream.

Cause: Heavy rainfall and construction flaws led to the failure of the dam, inundating nearby areas.

Consequences: At least 40 fatalities, with hundreds missing and thousands displaced. Villages were destroyed, and agricultural lands were submerged, causing economic hardship.

Measures Taken: Laos and neighboring countries reviewed dam safety protocols, with stricter regulations and inspection requirements. International support was provided for safer dam construction practices.

55. The 2023 Turkey–Syria Earthquake

Location and Date: February 6, 2023; Southeastern Turkey and Northwestern Syria

Event Details: A powerful 7.8 magnitude earthquake struck near the Turkish-Syrian border, followed by a series of aftershocks, devastating cities across both countries.

Cause: Movement along the East Anatolian Fault, a major tectonic boundary between the Anatolian and Arabian plates.

Consequences: Over 50,000 fatalities, hundreds of thousands injured, and widespread displacement. Entire neighborhoods and infrastructure, including historic sites, were reduced to rubble, and the humanitarian impact in Syria was worsened by ongoing conflict.

Measures Taken: Turkey has since worked to improve building codes and earthquake-resistant construction. International aid has focused on recovery efforts, while emergency response systems in both countries are being re-evaluated.

56. Cyclone Amphan

Location and Date: May 2020; Eastern India and Bangladesh, particularly the Sundarbans region
Event Details: A Category 5 cyclone that caused significant destruction across Eastern India and Bangladesh, including Kolkata.
Cause: Warm sea surface temperatures and favorable atmospheric conditions in the Bay of Bengal, with climate change likely intensifying its strength.
Consequences: Around 128 fatalities, severe displacement, and billions in damages to homes, infrastructure, and agriculture. Coastal ecosystems, especially the Sundarbans, were heavily impacted, threatening wildlife and local communities.
Measures Taken: India and Bangladesh improved cyclone shelters and early warning systems, expanded mangrove conservation to protect coastlines, and focused on building resilient infrastructure to withstand strong storms.

57. The 2020 Australian Bushfire Season ("Black Summer")

Location and Date: June 2019 – March 2020; primarily Southeastern Australia

Event Details: A series of catastrophic bushfires burned millions of acres, severely impacting communities, wildlife, and ecosystems.

Cause: Extreme drought, high temperatures, and strong winds fueled the fires, with climate change intensifying the fire season.

Consequences: 33 fatalities, an estimated 3 billion animals affected, and more than 3,000 homes destroyed. The economic costs were over $100 billion, with widespread effects on health and air quality across Australia.

Measures Taken: Australia has expanded its fire prevention strategies, increased funding for firefighting resources, and invested in forest management practices. Greater emphasis is being placed on climate adaptation to address fire risks.

58. The 2022 Tonga Volcanic Eruption and Tsunami

Location and Date: January 15, 2022; Hunga Tonga–Hunga Ha'apai, Tonga

Event Details: An underwater volcanic eruption caused a powerful tsunami, affecting Tonga and nearby islands, with shockwaves felt globally.

Cause: A submarine volcano erupted explosively, displacing massive amounts of seawater and sending ash into the atmosphere.

Consequences: Four fatalities, extensive destruction to homes and infrastructure, and communication disruptions due to undersea cable damage. Ashfall contaminated drinking water and affected agriculture.

Measures Taken: Tonga improved monitoring of volcanic activity and established protocols for rapid response to tsunamis. International aid supported infrastructure rebuilding and enhanced satellite-based communication to maintain contact in remote areas.

59. The 2021 Haiti Earthquake

Location and Date: August 14, 2021; near Les Cayes, Haiti

Event Details: A magnitude 7.2 earthquake hit Haiti, devastating towns in the country's southwest.

Cause: The earthquake occurred along the Enriquillo–Plantain Garden fault zone, the same fault system responsible for the 2010 earthquake.

Consequences: Over 2,200 fatalities, thousands of injuries, and around 130,000 homes destroyed or damaged. Haiti's recovery was hampered by political instability and pre-existing infrastructure challenges.

Measures Taken: Relief efforts focused on rebuilding earthquake-resistant structures. Haiti has been working to improve emergency response training, although limited resources and political challenges have slowed comprehensive reforms.

60. The 2021 Texas Power Crisis

Location and Date: February 2021; Texas, USA
Event Details: A historic winter storm caused extensive power outages across Texas, leaving millions without heat, electricity, and water for days.
Cause: An Arctic blast overwhelmed Texas's isolated power grid, which was not winterized for such extreme cold. Demand for heating spiked while frozen infrastructure reduced power supply.
Consequences: Over 200 fatalities, widespread property damage from burst pipes, and an estimated $195 billion in economic losses. Food and water shortages and infrastructure failures highlighted systemic weaknesses.
Measures Taken: Texas is working to winterize its grid, increase interconnections with other power grids, and improve weatherization of energy infrastructure. Regulatory changes require power companies to prepare for extreme weather.

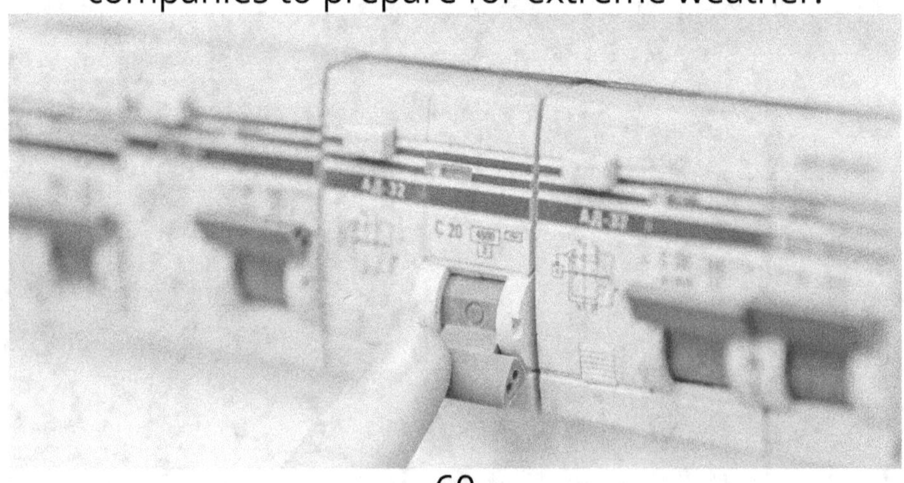

61. The 2006 Java Earthquake and Tsunami

Location and Date: July 17, 2006; Southern coast of Java, Indonesia

Event Details: A 7.7 magnitude earthquake triggered a local tsunami, impacting the coastal region of Pangandaran.

Cause: The earthquake originated along a fault in the Sunda megathrust zone, which runs parallel to Indonesia's southern coast.

Consequences: Approximately 668 fatalities, with significant damage to villages and tourist areas along the coast. The disaster displaced over 50,000 people.

Measures Taken: Indonesia expanded its tsunami warning systems and improved evacuation protocols. Local infrastructure was rebuilt with greater resilience, and educational programs raised awareness about tsunami safety.

62. The 2008 Mumbai Terror Attacks

Location and Date: November 26–29, 2008; Mumbai, India

Event Details: A series of coordinated terrorist attacks by armed gunmen targeted prominent locations in Mumbai, including hotels and a railway station.

Cause: Ten terrorists carried out an organized attack, taking hostages and spreading fear across the city. Investigations linked the attackers to militant groups.

Consequences: 174 fatalities, including civilians, police, and the attackers, with hundreds injured. The attacks caused major disruptions in India's financial capital and had a profound psychological impact.

Measures Taken: India enhanced counter-terrorism measures, established National Security Guards units in major cities, and increased intelligence-sharing. Surveillance and security at public venues were also intensified.

63. The 2011 Thailand Floods

Location and Date: July 2011 – January 2012; Central Thailand, including Bangkok

Event Details: Monsoon rains led to severe flooding across Thailand, particularly impacting Bangkok and surrounding industrial areas.

Cause: Continuous monsoon rains, compounded by poor water management and encroachment on floodplains, led to widespread inundation.

Consequences: Over 800 fatalities, with economic losses exceeding $45 billion. The floods disrupted supply chains, especially in the electronics and automotive sectors, impacting global markets.

Measures Taken: Thailand invested in flood management, including the construction of reservoirs and flood diversion channels. Urban planning policies now restrict development in natural floodplains, and early warning systems were strengthened.

64. The 2018 Sulawesi Tsunami and Liquefaction

Location and Date: September 28, 2018; Palu, Central Sulawesi, Indonesia

Event Details: A 7.5 magnitude earthquake triggered a local tsunami and liquefaction in Palu, causing massive destruction.

Cause: Tectonic movement along the Palu-Koro fault, with liquefaction turning soil into a slurry that engulfed homes and buildings.

Consequences: Over 4,300 fatalities, with thousands displaced and extensive damage to infrastructure, homes, and the Palu economy.

Measures Taken: Indonesia increased monitoring for both tsunamis and liquefaction-prone areas. Reconstruction efforts included building earthquake and liquefaction-resistant structures, and local education on evacuation procedures was enhanced.

65. The 2021 European Floods

Location and Date: July 2021; primarily Germany, Belgium, and the Netherlands

Event Details: Catastrophic flooding occurred after record rainfall in Western Europe, devastating cities and communities.

Cause: A stationary weather pattern brought intense rainfall, with climate change increasing the frequency and severity of such events.

Consequences: Over 220 fatalities, with damages exceeding $13 billion. Homes, infrastructure, and businesses were destroyed, and thousands were evacuated.

Measures Taken: Germany and Belgium have worked to improve flood defenses, reinforce riverbanks, and establish early warning systems. Climate adaptation measures, including flood-resilient urban planning, were prioritized.

66. The 2008 China Snowstorms

Location and Date: January–February 2008; primarily Southern China

Event Details: Severe snowstorms caused extensive disruption across Southern China during one of the busiest travel times, the Lunar New Year.

Cause: Unusually cold weather, exacerbated by a La Niña event, led to heavy snow and ice, affecting areas unprepared for winter conditions.

Consequences: 129 fatalities, with millions stranded or displaced due to transport disruptions. Widespread power outages and economic losses estimated at $21 billion.

Measures Taken: China invested in winter preparedness infrastructure, particularly in the power sector, and improved emergency response systems for severe winter weather.

67. The 2013 Bohol Earthquake

Location and Date: October 15, 2013; Bohol, Philippines

Event Details: A magnitude 7.2 earthquake struck the island of Bohol, causing widespread destruction to homes, roads, and historical landmarks.

Cause: The earthquake occurred due to tectonic activity along the East Bohol Fault.

Consequences: Around 222 fatalities, 976 injuries, and over 73,000 structures damaged or destroyed, including centuries-old churches. Many people were displaced, and economic losses were significant.

Measures Taken: The Philippines implemented stricter building codes, expanded earthquake monitoring, and improved emergency preparedness in high-risk areas. Awareness campaigns were conducted to educate communities on safety during earthquakes.

68. The 2020 Nashville Tornadoes

Location and Date: March 2–3, 2020; Tennessee, USA
Event Details: A series of powerful tornadoes tore through Nashville and surrounding areas, causing severe destruction.
Cause: A strong storm system produced multiple tornadoes, with high wind speeds reaching EF3 and EF4 levels.
Consequences: 25 fatalities, hundreds injured, and extensive damage to homes, businesses, and schools. The economic loss was significant, and thousands were left without power.
Measures Taken: Tennessee invested in better tornado warning systems, strengthened building codes for resilience against high winds, and promoted community tornado preparedness programs.

69. The 2017 Sri Lanka Floods and Landslides

Location and Date: May 2017; Southern and Western Sri Lanka

Event Details: Monsoon rains triggered widespread flooding and landslides, affecting Sri Lanka's densely populated coastal areas.

Cause: Heavy rainfall during the monsoon season, exacerbated by deforestation and unplanned urban expansion in flood-prone areas.

Consequences: 224 fatalities, significant displacement, and extensive damage to homes, infrastructure, and agriculture. The economic cost reached over $1.5 billion.

Measures Taken: Sri Lanka enhanced flood management infrastructure, implemented stricter land-use policies, and promoted reforestation efforts to reduce landslide risks.

70. The 2016 Ecuador Earthquake

Location and Date: April 16, 2016; Coastal Ecuador, near Manta and Portoviejo

Event Details: A magnitude 7.8 earthquake struck the Ecuadorian coast, causing widespread damage.

Cause: Movement along the convergent boundary between the Nazca and South American plates triggered the earthquake.

Consequences: Approximately 676 fatalities, thousands injured, and significant infrastructure and economic losses. Many buildings and roads were destroyed, impacting Ecuador's tourism and economy.

Measures Taken: Ecuador improved building standards for earthquake resilience, expanded its seismic monitoring network, and invested in public awareness campaigns on earthquake safety.

71. The 2018 Indonesia Earthquake and Tsunami

Location and Date: September 28, 2018; Palu, Central Sulawesi, Indonesia

Event Details: A 7.5 magnitude earthquake caused a tsunami that hit the coast of Palu, along with liquefaction that devastated the region.

Cause: Tectonic movement along the Palu-Koro fault.

Consequences: Over 4,300 fatalities, with extensive infrastructure destruction and widespread displacement. Economic losses impacted the local economy, and thousands were left homeless.

Measures Taken: Indonesia expanded its early warning systems and invested in tsunami monitoring and emergency preparedness, particularly for coastal regions vulnerable to tsunamis and liquefaction.

72. The 2017 California Wine Country Fires

Location and Date: October 2017; Northern California, USA

Event Details: A series of wildfires burned through Napa, Sonoma, and surrounding counties, affecting California's wine-producing regions.

Cause: Prolonged drought and high winds created extreme fire conditions, and power line malfunctions contributed to the ignition.

Consequences: 44 fatalities, over 8,000 structures destroyed, and billions in damages. The fires heavily impacted California's wine industry, and air quality deteriorated across the region.

Measures Taken: California utility companies updated equipment and developed shutoff policies during high fire risk. Investments were made in wildfire prevention, forest management, and community preparedness programs.

73. Cyclone Idai and Cyclone Kenneth

Location and Date: March and April 2019; primarily Mozambique, Malawi, and Zimbabwe

Event Details: Cyclone Idai, one of the worst tropical cyclones to hit the Southern Hemisphere, was followed by Cyclone Kenneth just six weeks later.

Cause: Warm ocean waters intensified both cyclones in the Indian Ocean, causing high wind speeds and catastrophic flooding.

Consequences: Idai caused over 1,300 fatalities and widespread damage in Mozambique, with Cyclone Kenneth causing additional destruction. Millions were displaced, and food insecurity increased due to destroyed crops.

Measures Taken: International aid focused on rebuilding efforts, and Mozambique worked on improving flood resilience and cyclone preparedness. Local governments invested in better early warning systems and coastal defenses.

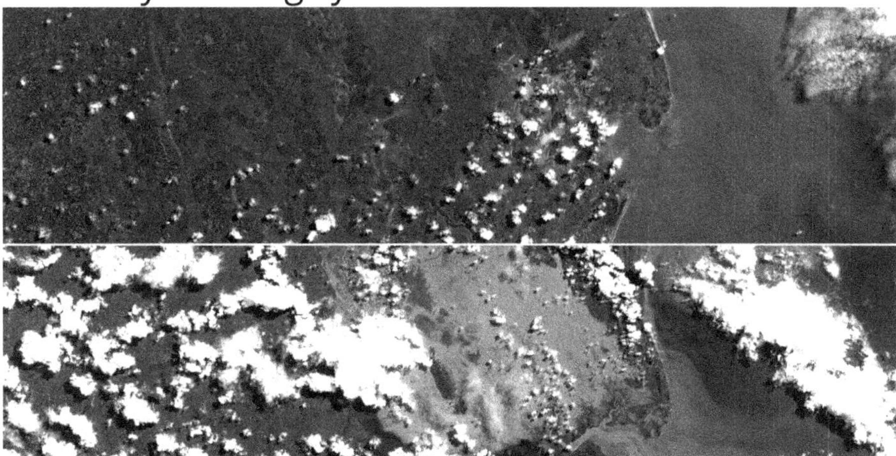

74. The 2020 Hurricane Laura

Location and Date: August 2020; primarily Louisiana and Texas, USA

Event Details: A Category 4 hurricane that made landfall in Louisiana, causing widespread wind damage and flooding.

Cause: Warm waters in the Gulf of Mexico fueled Laura's rapid intensification.

Consequences: 77 fatalities, over $19 billion in damages, and extensive property and infrastructure destruction. Many homes and businesses in coastal and inland areas were affected.

Measures Taken: Louisiana and Texas invested in stronger building codes, expanded flood mitigation infrastructure, and improved hurricane preparedness campaigns for residents.

75. The 2019 Venice Floods

Location and Date: November 2019; Venice, Italy
Event Details: Venice experienced some of the worst flooding in decades, with water levels reaching nearly two meters, submerging much of the city.
Cause: High tides and storm surges, worsened by climate change and Venice's subsidence, led to the flooding.
Consequences: Significant damage to historical sites, businesses, and homes. The economic impact was estimated at over $1 billion.
Measures Taken: The MOSE project, a floodgate system, was activated to protect Venice from future high tides. Venice also developed emergency plans to safeguard cultural heritage sites from flooding.

76. The 2018 Kerala Floods

Location and Date: August 2018; Kerala, India
Event Details: Exceptionally heavy monsoon rains led to flooding and landslides across Kerala, affecting nearly all districts.
Cause: Extreme rainfall combined with inadequate dam management and deforestation in hill areas.
Consequences: Over 480 fatalities, severe displacement, and an economic cost exceeding $4 billion. Thousands of homes were destroyed, and infrastructure and agriculture were badly affected.
Measures Taken: Kerala invested in improved flood forecasting systems, dam management, and community training on flood response. Policies were introduced to promote sustainable land-use and water management.

77. The 2022 Japan Heatwave

Location and Date: June 2022; primarily Tokyo and surrounding regions, Japan

Event Details: Japan experienced record-breaking heat, with temperatures reaching highs of 40°C (104°F) in Tokyo.

Cause: An atmospheric high-pressure system trapped warm air over Japan, with climate change contributing to the intensity and frequency of heatwaves.

Consequences: Increased health risks, particularly among the elderly, with thousands treated for heat-related illnesses. Agricultural production was impacted, and power demand surged, leading to supply concerns.

Measures Taken: Japan expanded its public health campaigns for heat safety, increased cooling center access, and strengthened energy grid resilience for high-demand periods. The government has invested in climate adaptation to mitigate future heatwave effects.

78. The 2019 Amazon Fires

Location and Date: August–October 2019; Amazon rainforest, primarily in Brazil

Event Details: Large areas of the Amazon rainforest burned due to fires set for land clearing, causing concern about deforestation and environmental impacts.

Cause: Deforestation, agricultural expansion, and land-clearing practices, exacerbated by dry conditions.

Consequences: Massive loss of biodiversity, harm to indigenous communities, and significant carbon emissions. The fires sparked international concern and calls to protect the Amazon.

Measures Taken: Brazil increased monitoring and enforcement of deforestation regulations, and international conservation organizations stepped in with support. Initiatives to promote sustainable agriculture and reforestation have expanded.

79. The 2014 Balkan Floods

Location and Date: May 2014; primarily Serbia, Bosnia and Herzegovina, and Croatia

Event Details: Record-breaking rainfall led to severe flooding and landslides, impacting several Balkan countries.

Cause: A stationary low-pressure system brought continuous rain to the region, with climate change likely playing a role in the intensity of the storm.

Consequences: Over 80 fatalities, displacement of 1.6 million people, and billions in economic losses. Flooding devastated communities, agriculture, and infrastructure.

Measures Taken: The affected countries improved flood defenses, invested in water management systems, and launched cross-border cooperation for flood preparedness and emergency response.

80. The 2021 German Floods (Ahr Valley and Rhine Basin)

Location and Date: July 2021; Western Germany, Belgium, and parts of the Netherlands

Event Details: Heavy rainfall led to catastrophic flooding across Western Europe, with Germany's Ahr Valley among the worst-hit areas.

Cause: A slow-moving low-pressure system led to extreme rain, with climate change likely increasing the severity and frequency of such events.

Consequences: Over 220 fatalities, extensive infrastructure damage, and economic losses estimated at €10 billion. Roads, railways, and homes were swept away, and several towns were severely impacted.

Measures Taken: Germany invested in flood-resistant infrastructure, improved early warning systems, and developed riverbank fortification projects. There has also been increased emphasis on climate adaptation strategies across Europe.

81. The 2010 Eyjafjallajökull Eruption

Location and Date: April 2010; Iceland
Event Details: The eruption of Eyjafjallajökull volcano sent ash clouds across Europe, causing massive air travel disruptions.
Cause: Volcanic activity beneath a glacier, which melted ice, increasing ash production and sending fine ash particles high into the atmosphere.
Consequences: Thousands of flights were canceled, impacting over 10 million passengers and costing the aviation industry over $1.7 billion. Economic impacts were also felt in related industries like tourism and shipping.
Measures Taken: European countries improved volcanic ash monitoring and developed protocols for air traffic management during volcanic events. Research into volcanic plume behavior was prioritized to better assess risks.

82. The 2021 Congo Mount Nyiragongo Eruption

Location and Date: May 22, 2021; Goma, Democratic Republic of Congo

Event Details: Mount Nyiragongo erupted, sending lava flows toward Goma and causing mass evacuations.

Cause: The eruption was part of the volcanic activity of the East African Rift.

Consequences: 31 fatalities, thousands displaced, and significant damage to homes and infrastructure. Ash and toxic gases impacted public health, and seismic activity continued to threaten the area.

Measures Taken: The DRC improved monitoring of Nyiragongo and surrounding volcanoes, and evacuation plans for Goma were refined. International aid helped establish early warning systems, and educational campaigns focused on volcanic safety.

83. The 2004 Sumatra–Andaman Earthquake and Tsunami

Location and Date: December 26, 2004; Indian Ocean, affecting Indonesia, Thailand, Sri Lanka, India, and other coastal nations

Event Details: A 9.1–9.3 magnitude undersea earthquake triggered a devastating tsunami across the Indian Ocean.

Cause: The Indian plate subducting beneath the Burma plate caused a rupture, releasing massive energy and creating the tsunami.

Consequences: Over 230,000 fatalities across multiple countries, with millions displaced and extensive destruction to coastal areas. Economic losses were in the billions, and entire communities were lost to the waves.

Measures Taken: The Indian Ocean Tsunami Warning and Mitigation System (IOTWMS) was established, featuring seismic monitoring and early warning systems across vulnerable countries.

84. The 2011 Christchurch Earthquake

Location and Date: February 22, 2011; Christchurch, New Zealand

Event Details: A 6.2 magnitude earthquake struck Christchurch, causing extensive structural damage in the city center.

Cause: Movement along a previously unknown fault in the region of Canterbury.

Consequences: 185 fatalities, thousands injured, and significant damage to buildings and infrastructure. Many historic structures were damaged or lost, and the economic impact reached around $40 billion.

Measures Taken: New Zealand updated building codes to improve earthquake resilience and established stricter construction requirements. Emergency response protocols and community preparedness were strengthened.

85. The 2017 Sierra Leone Mudslide

Location and Date: August 14, 2017; Freetown, Sierra Leone

Event Details: Intense rainfall caused a massive mudslide in the Regent area of Freetown, burying homes and communities.

Cause: Deforestation, unregulated building on hillsides, and heavy rainfall increased soil instability, leading to the landslide.

Consequences: Over 1,100 fatalities, with thousands displaced and significant damage to homes and infrastructure.

Measures Taken: Sierra Leone developed land-use regulations to prevent building on unstable slopes and initiated reforestation efforts. Emergency response protocols were enhanced, and communities were educated about landslide risks.

86. The 2016 Hurricane Matthew

Location and Date: October 2016; Caribbean and Southeastern USA, particularly Haiti
Event Details: A Category 5 hurricane, Matthew caused widespread destruction, particularly in Haiti, which was already vulnerable from previous natural disasters.
Cause: Warm Atlantic waters fueled Matthew, allowing it to reach maximum strength as it swept through the Caribbean.
Consequences: Over 500 fatalities, significant destruction of homes and infrastructure, and widespread crop losses. In Haiti, thousands were left homeless, with waterborne diseases increasing due to poor sanitation.
Measures Taken: Haiti received international aid for rebuilding and disease prevention, and the country improved emergency management practices. The U.S. and Caribbean nations strengthened hurricane warning systems and implemented community evacuation plans.

87. The 2011 Japan Earthquake and Tsunami (Tohoku)

Location and Date: March 11, 2011; Japan

Event Details: A magnitude 9.1 earthquake triggered a massive tsunami that struck Japan's northeastern coast, resulting in the Fukushima nuclear disaster.

Cause: Subduction of the Pacific Plate beneath the North American Plate along the Japan Trench.

Consequences: Over 15,000 fatalities, with widespread displacement and extensive damage to infrastructure and industry. The Fukushima nuclear plant meltdown prompted long-term evacuation zones.

Measures Taken: Japan implemented extensive tsunami defenses and nuclear safety protocols. Enhanced building codes were established for earthquake resilience, and international nuclear standards were updated.

88. The 2005 Hurricane Katrina

Location and Date: August 23–31, 2005; U.S. Gulf Coast, especially New Orleans

Event Details: Hurricane Katrina, a Category 5 storm, caused severe flooding and destruction in New Orleans after levees failed.

Cause: Warm waters in the Gulf of Mexico intensified Katrina, with storm surges overwhelming the levee system.

Consequences: Over 1,800 fatalities, extensive property damage, and displacement of hundreds of thousands. The economic impact was estimated at over $125 billion.

Measures Taken: The U.S. Army Corps of Engineers strengthened New Orleans's levee system, and FEMA reformed disaster response practices. Community preparedness and flood defenses across the Gulf Coast were reinforced.

89. The 2021 Texas Freeze

Location and Date: February 13–17, 2021; Texas, USA
Event Details: An unprecedented winter storm hit Texas, leading to massive power outages, water shortages, and infrastructure collapse.
Cause: A polar vortex brought unusually cold temperatures, with Texas's independent power grid failing to meet demand due to inadequate weatherization.
Consequences: Over 200 fatalities and an estimated $195 billion in economic losses due to burst pipes, food shortages, and damages to homes.
Measures Taken: Texas mandated the winterization of power plants, increased grid interconnections, and strengthened weatherization standards to prevent similar infrastructure failures.

90. The 2020 Hurricane Iota and Eta (Double Impact)

Location and Date: November 2020; Central America, particularly Honduras and Nicaragua
Event Details: Two back-to-back Category 4 and 5 hurricanes devastated Central America within two weeks.
Cause: Warm Caribbean waters and climate variability intensified both hurricanes, increasing rainfall and wind damage.
Consequences: Over 200 fatalities, thousands displaced, and billions in economic losses. Infrastructure, homes, and agriculture were heavily impacted, creating long-term recovery challenges.
Measures Taken: Central American countries improved hurricane shelters, early warning systems, and invested in flood-resilient infrastructure. International aid focused on rebuilding efforts, climate resilience, and emergency preparedness.

Final Reflections

As we close this journey through some of the world's most devastating cataclysms, we are left with a deeper understanding of the delicate balance that sustains life on Earth. From the fury of nature to the consequences of human ambition and error, these events highlight the forces that both create and destroy, shaping the landscapes of our world and the resilience of our societies.

Each disaster chronicled in Shadows of Destruction is more than just a historical account. It's a story of lives interrupted, of cities reborn, and of humanity's remarkable ability to adapt in the face of adversity. We have seen how earthquakes can shatter entire cities in moments, how volcanic eruptions can alter global climates, and how industrial disasters can transform our understanding of safety and responsibility. But we have also witnessed the remarkable progress that arises from such tragedy: better building codes, more sophisticated early warning systems, scientific advances, and a collective commitment to preventing future catastrophes.

These lessons are particularly critical today. As climate change accelerates, many of these natural hazards are intensifying in scale and frequency. Hurricanes grow stronger, wildfires rage longer, and rising seas threaten our coastal cities. At the same time, our rapidly urbanizing and interconnected world increases the risk of human-made disasters, from industrial spills to infrastructure failures. Now, more than ever, we are challenged to apply the wisdom earned through past events to build a safer, more resilient world.

Throughout this book, we have seen not only the raw power of these cataclysms but also the strength and resilience of the human spirit. Communities around the world have rebuilt from the ashes of disaster, honoring lost lives by making profound changes to protect future generations. We have witnessed the global efforts to prepare, mitigate, and respond to disasters through collaboration, innovation, and the sheer will to survive.

As we look to the future, Shadows of Destruction reminds us that while we cannot eliminate all risks, we have the power to reduce them. We have the tools, the knowledge, and the empathy to forge solutions that respect both the natural world and the people who inhabit it. Let these stories of destruction and resilience be a testament to the strength of humanity and a call to action for each of us to play a part in protecting the planet and one another.

In a world that will continue to face challenges, may we carry forward the lessons learned from these shadows of destruction. May we honor those who suffered and rebuild with a renewed commitment to resilience, compassion, and shared responsibility.

And may we remember that while nature's forces
are often beyond our control, our response to them
is within our power, shaping the world we leave
behind for generations to come.

93